Indian Nations

THE ZUNI

by
Edmund J. Ladd

General Editors
Herman J. Viola and Felix C. Lowe

A Rivilo Book

RAINTREE
STECK-VAUGHN
RSVP PUBLISHERS

A Harcourt Company

Austin · New York
www.steck-vaughn.com

Dedicated to the memory of the author, Edmund J. Ladd

Published by Raintree Steck-Vaughn Publishers, an imprint of the Steck-Vaughn Company

Developed for Steck-Vaughn Company by Rivilo Books

Editors: David Jeffery and David Stern

Photo Research: Linda Sykes

Design: Barbara Lisenby and Todd Hirshman

Electronic Preparation: Lyda Guz

Raintree Steck-Vaughn Publishers Staff

Publishing Director: Walter Kossmann

Editor: Kathy DeVico

Electronic Production: Scott Melcer

Cover: Zuni Olla maidens balance traditional pottery on their heads at Gallup Inter-tribal Indian Ceremonial, in Gallup, New Mexico.

Photo Credits: Chuck Place: cover, pp. 25 bottom right, 27, 28; Victoria and Julius Lisi: illustration, pp. 4, 6; Stephen Trimble: pp. 7, 14 top and bottom, 24 top (Heard Museum), 38, 39; Adam Woolfit/Corbis: p. 8; David Muench: p. 10; Tom Bean/Corbis: p. 11; National Park Service: p. 12–13; Jesse Nusbaum, courtesy Museum of New Mexico: pp. 15 (negative #61730), 23 top (negative #43170); Ben Wittick, courtesy Museum of New Mexico: pp. 16 (negative #16415), 35 (negative #16010); Courtesy Museum of New Mexico (negative #99596): p. 17; Bruce Elliot, courtesy Museum of New Mexico (negative #140788): p. 19 left; Frederick Maude, courtesy Museum of New Mexico (negative #10391): p. 19 right; Michael Mouchette/©1984 Zuni Arts and Crafts, courtesy Dale Anderson/Aztec Media: p. 20 left; John Running: pp. 20 right, 22 bottom, 32 bottom; Corbis: p. 21; ©1999 Wendy Fontenelle/A:shiwia:wan Museum and Heritage Center, Zuni Pueblo: pp. 22 top, 25 bottom left, 37; Corbis Bettmann: p. 23 bottom; Corbis: p. 24 bottom; Dave Houser/Corbis: p. 25 top right; Pat Vasquez-Cunningham/AP Wide World: p. 26; Dale Anderson/ Aztec Media: pp. 29, 31; Pueblo of Zuni Arts and Crafts ©1990/photo courtesy Dale Anderson/Aztec Media: p. 32 top; Timothy O'Sullivan, courtesy Museum of New Mexico (negative #40197): p. 34; AP/Wide World: p. 36; National Anthropological Archives/National Museum of Natural History/Smithsonian Institution (negative #84-7544): p. 42.

Library of Congress Cataloging-in-Publication-Data

Ladd, Edmund J.

    The Zuni/by Edmund J. Ladd.

       p.   cm. — (Indian nations)

    Includes bibliographical references and index.

    Summary: Introduces the history, culture, religion, family life, and tribal government of the Zuni people.

    ISBN 0-8172-5454-4

    1. Zuni Indians — Juvenile literature. [1. Zuni Indians.

    2. Indians of North America — New Mexico.]   I. Title. II. Series.

E99.Z9L35   2000

978.9'004979 — dc21   99-23362

                                                     CIP

Printed and bound in the United States of America

1 2 3 4 5 6 7 8 9 0 LB 03 02 01 00

Contents

Creation Story

Fables such as "Turkey Girl" (see page 7) are told mainly in the dark of wintertime to teach children lessons and to entertain them. But the Zuni creation story—"the word of the beginning"—is believed to be a true historical account. It can be told during any season:

According to the elders, in ancient times there were no humans in the world. The days were empty. There was no singing, no joy, no dancing, no prayers, and no gifts.

Every day Sun Father rose in the East to bring a new morning. When he sank into the western ocean, it became night. Every day, as Sun Father traveled high above Mother Earth, he could hear the cries of his children deep in her womb. One day, as he passed above, he saw two columns of foam at the base of a waterfall. With his great power, he put life into the columns of foam. These two columns became the "Twin Gods."

Sun Father said to the Twin Gods, "Go into the womb of Mother Earth and bring forth my children to my light and warmth." The Twins obeyed. After many tries of diving into the world of darkness, they brought forth the People up to this world. The Zunis were thus born of Mother Earth and Sun Father.

The Zuni traveled for many years in search of the "Center Place" in which to live. Then the elders asked the help of Water Spider. They asked him to reach out to the four corners of the world with his long legs. Where his heart came to rest would be

◀ *Sun Father gives life to two columns of foam from a waterfall. The Twin Gods he creates father the People.*

the Center Place. Water Spider did so, and his heart came to rest at the present day Zuni Pueblo, **Jalona:itiwanna**.

These are the Zuni tribal oral traditions: Led by the Twin Gods, the Zuni emerged from the depths of darkness to the light and warmth of Sun Father and the present world. This "Word of the Beginning" explains all aspects of life. It also explains the Zuni view of the world: their sense of time, colors, space, numbers, directions—and spiritual properties of life, death, and the hereafter.

"Turkey Girl"

Many years ago, when our grandfathers were still living at Kyaki'ma, at the south end of Towayallane (Corn Mountain), there was a poor, young Zuni girl who was responsible for taking care of the village turkeys. Her feet were bare; her dress was tattered and worn; her hair had never been brushed. But she was happy with her friends, the turkeys.

Every day she herded them to the best feeding grounds. Every evening she took them to their pens and sheltered them. After her dinner, she would curl up in bed and fall asleep listening to the soft gobbling of her friends.

One day, as she was moving the turkeys to their feeding grounds, she heard the sound of drums. The drumming meant the "holding hands" dance was to happen in the village that night. The girl tried to pretend that she did not care about the dance. But as she listened to the drums, tears began to fall down her face, softly at first, then in a great flood.

"Why is our little mother sad?" a deep, melodious voice asked.

The girl looked up and saw the Tom Turkey standing before her.

A view of Towayallane (Corn Mountain), looking east from the center of the village. Turkey Girl's home was at the south end.

7

"Have we done something to make her unhappy?" the Tom Turkey asked.

"You are speaking!" the girl gasped, her eyes wide in surprise. "I did not know you could speak the human language."

"We hear and understand all human speech," said the turkey. "But since the Twin Gods have hidden our tongues, we are not allowed to speak openly. Are you sad because you wish that you could go to the holding hands dance?"

"It is true," the girl admitted.

"Then follow me."

The Tom Turkey led the girl into a clearing where the flock of turkeys had assembled. He stood in the center and spoke: "Because our mother has been good to us all, she will get her wish. We will prepare for the dance."

The turkeys all gathered around the girl. In a fast, shuffling motion, they began to dance around her, faster and faster, until all was just a blur of dust and feathers.

The cloud of dust and feathers settled. The girl let out a small cry of delight. She could not believe her eyes! In place of her castoff clothes, she was now wearing the traditional dress of a young Zuni maiden.

Once again the Tom Turkey spoke: "Now go and enjoy

A modern Zuni girl dressed in traditional fabrics and jewelry. She reminds us of Turkey Girl, whose shabby clothes were made glorious by her dancing turkeys.

yourself at the dance—but remember one thing. Do not stay beyond sunset. Do you understand?"

"Yes, I do," the girl said, barely able to contain her excitement. Off she went, over the trail to the village.

The **yaaya**, or holding-hands dance, was in full swing. As she approached the plaza, all the young men stared at her. They wondered who she was and what village she had come from.

Before she knew it, two young men had taken hold of her hands, and she, too, was dancing! All afternoon, she danced with one young man after another. She was having so much fun, she lost track of the time. Then she looked up in the sky. Sun Father was just two fingers above the horizon and about to enter his western home!

She ran out of the plaza, racing toward her turkey friends as fast as she could. But her beautiful clothes all fell away, and she was once again barefoot, wearing tattered clothing. As she ran toward the turkey flock, she called for them to wait. But they landed on a big flat rock, and flew off into the night to become the wild turkeys of today.

Because the Earth was newly formed and still soft, you can still see the turkey tracks on the rock they landed on. It is called "tone a:teana:wa"—the place of the turkey tracks. (The symbol ":" in a word means to draw out the vowel sound when pronouncing it: Tone-aaaa teana-aaaa wa.)

Prehistory

The earliest human use of the Zuni region in what is now southwestern New Mexico dates back to the "Paleo-Indian" period, about 5,000 years before Christ (5000 B.C.). The Paleo-Indian people are known mostly from the large stone spearheads they left behind. These people, perhaps in small family groups, traveled from place to place following big game animals. The people were mainly meat-eaters, stopping now and then to gather wild plants, but they had no permanent towns or villages.

During the early part of the "Archaic" period, from about 5000 to 2500 B.C., the people still largely depended on hunting

A prehistoric petroglyph, or a carving on stone, of the Sun may have been made by ancestors of the Zuni.

and gathering wild plants. In about 2500 B.C., agriculture was introduced from Mexico. Zuni first planted corn, and later beans and squash. By the end of the Archaic era, most of the people had become farmers.

The period from A.D. 1 to A.D. 1539 saw many changes. Pithouses, or wood and mud structures dug into the ground, began to appear among the Zuni. The people started to congregate into larger groups, creating villages. With the introduction of pottery, ceremonial clothing, and large, aboveground stone masonry structures, Zuni culture began to blossom.

Sometime before the year 1500, the people of the region all gathered into six large villages. They called themselves the **A:shiwi** (the name cannot be translated). By this time, they had developed their own language, as well as a wide-ranging network of trade connections.

Spaniards, who first arrived in the area in the middle of the 16th century, called the valley the A:shiwi lived in the Suni (Zuni) valley. Thus, they labeled its inhabitants the Zuni Indians.

*Ruins of ancient Zuni buildings made of mud bricks. They stand on top of a **mesa** at El Moro National Monument, in New Mexico.*

Key Historical Events

Encounters with Spain

The first recorded encounter between the A:shiwi and Westerners occurred in 1539. A dark-skinned Moroccan named Esteban arrived at the pueblo (dwelling) of **Hawikuh**, the southernmost of the six A:shiwi villages. Esteban was a slave of the **viceroy** of New Spain and an advance scout for Fray (Spanish for "Father") Marcos de Niza, a Franciscan priest. Some historical accounts say that Esteban attacked the A:shiwi women. Others say the Zuni attacked him while he was trying to escape their village. In any case, he was killed. Though Fray Marcos never entered the A:shiwi village, he returned to Mexico City claiming that he saw "great and rich towns."

The priest's stories started a gold rush, as Spaniards went in search of whatever might be valuable. In 1540 Francisco Vásquez de Coronado led the first full-scale expedition into the land of the A:shiwi. On July 7, 1540, he defeated the A:shiwi

in the first battle the tribe ever fought. Coronado found no gold, though. Two years later he returned to Mexico City with empty pockets and an empty heart.

Forty years passed before Spaniards returned. Fray Augustin Rodriguez and Francisco Sanchez Chamuscado left the province of Chihuahua, Mexico, in June 1581 and briefly visited the "Suni" valley. They came in peace, so they were well received by the A:shiwi.

A year later Antonio de Espejo led another exploration party from northern Chihuahua to the valley. He reached the village of Ma'zakya on March 14, 1583. For the next three months, his party took over rooms and ate food supplied by the people at **Jalona:wa**, Hawikuh, and Ma'zakya.

Conquest and Revolt

On April 30, 1598, a Spanish colonist named Juan de Oñate took possession of all the lands and kingdoms north of the Rio Grande River "in the name of the king of Spain." The Rio Grande was the border between Mexico and what is now Texas.

A column of volunteer Spaniards marched out from Mexico City in 1539 to support Francisco Vásquez de Coronado. He led the first major Spanish expedition into the land of the Zuni. This was the first battle that the Zuni fought.

In 1598 Juan de Oñate led a large group of colonists across the Rio Grande River into Zuni Country. Along the way they stopped at the wall of a mesa (left) and carved notice of their presence in stone (below).

Oñate led a great expedition of soldiers, farmers, and religious missionaries into what is now New Mexico.

Oñate's expedition brought useful items such as metal tools, harnesses, oxcarts, and medicinal plants to the A:shiwi. The people gladly accepted these. But the Spaniards also brought a new language, a new religion, and a new civil government. These the A:shiwi resisted.

In 1680 an all-out war began between Native Americans throughout the Southwest and the Spanish intruders. The A:shiwi burned Spanish churches, killed soldiers and priests, and retreated to Towayallane, or Corn Mountain, their mountain fortress. But the Spaniards were too numerous and too powerful. In 1698 Diego de Vargas led a "bloodless reconquest" of the Zuni people. They came down from Towayallane and settled in one village, which they now called "Zuni Pueblo."

The A:shiwi remained a self-sufficient people underneath Spanish rule. Keeping their ancient traditions, but taking what they found useful from the invading culture, the people passed the next two centuries in relative peace.

For many generations the A:shiwi people followed traditional ways. This woman bakes bread in a Spanish-style oven made of mud brick.

Encounters with the United States

Unlike many other Native American tribes, the Zuni were never at war with the United States. The Treaty of Guadalupe Hidalgo in 1848 made New Mexico a part of the United States. In that same year, the Zuni Governor negotiated "Articles of Confederation" with U. S. Army Colonel H. P. Boyakin. These "Articles" promised that "Zuni shall be Protected in the full management of all its rights of private Property and Religion."

In 1850 representatives from the Zuni tribe traveled to Santa Fe. There, on August 8th, they signed an agreement with U.S. Indian Agent James S. Calhoun, which promised protection of tribal land as well as self-government. The first Zuni reservation was established in 1877. Though this reservation was much smaller than their prehistoric hunting grounds, it was larger than the territory the Spanish had granted them.

During the 19th century, much of the North American continent was being colonized. European settlers moved westward, and missionaries divided the territory for their Christianizing efforts. The United States military established many roads for

In 1897 U.S. soldiers camped in front of the Zuni Pueblo when they were surveying the country for new roads.

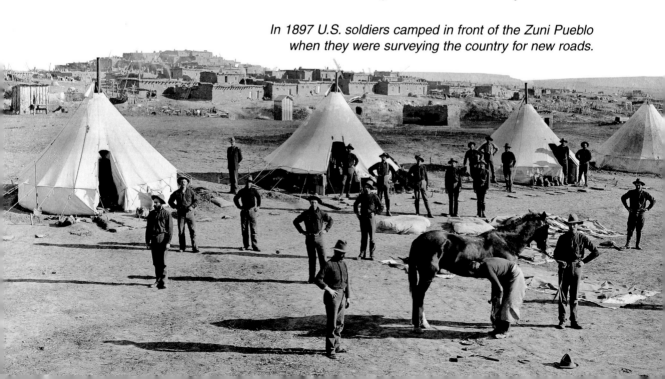

cross-country travel, and the intercontinental railroad system was built. Zuni Pueblo would have been a rail center but for the discovery of large coal deposits in present day Gallup, New Mexico. The railroad passed through that town instead.

Attempts to "Americanize" Indians included boarding schools. Here at Black Rock, New Mexico, in about 1910, discipline was strict.

The Bureau of Indian Affairs opened the first Day School on the Zuni reservation in 1898. In 1907 the Black Rock Boarding School was opened. On November 21, 1934, the Zuni people voted to have popular elections to elect their tribal officials.

Way of Life

Despite invasions by Spaniards and Mexicans from the south and Americans from the east, the Zuni have been very selective in what they have allowed to become part of their culture. Up until the end of the 1800s, they were economically self-sufficient. Today they still maintain their own religion, their own language, and are governed under a modified Zuni-Spanish-American constitution.

The Zuni reservation is located in southwestern New Mexico. It consists of Zuni Pueblo, as well as four farming

About 9,000 people live on the Zuni Reservation today. It consists of the Zuni Pueblo and four farming villages. The nearest large town is Gallup, New Mexico.

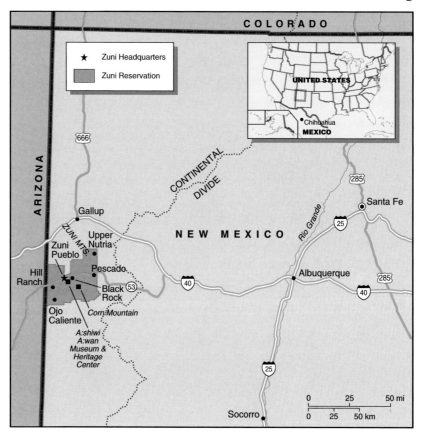

18

villages established in the early 1800s. The four villages are Nutria (so named because the Spanish found a small, beaver-like animal, the nutria, in the area), Pescado, (because the Spanish found many fish in the small stream), Hill Ranch (Tekapo), and Ojo Caliente (hot springs).

Clothing

Before the arrival of the Spaniards, Zuni clothing was very simple. Women wore an outer garment of cotton with a belt, and in warm weather, moccasins or sandals. In the winter, they wore shoes made from rabbit skins, with the fur on the inside. Men dressed in leggings made of woven cotton and a loose shirt. Both men and women wore woven indigo blue socks or "foot warmers" in the winter and summer.

Small children wore no clothing. Older children wore very loose-fitting shirts. Men and women had bangs and wore their hair tied in a bundle behind the neck with a short woven belt. Men also often wore a scarf tied around the head. In the winter, Zuni used woven rabbit fur or turkey feather blankets to keep warm.

After the Pueblo Revolt of 1680, styles changed. Yarn goods from Mexico, leather shoes and rawhide for moccasins, and wool

In about 1895 a grandfather dressed in cotton clothing (right) carried his grandson who, like many small children, wore no clothes in summer. By 1920, Zuni women might wear fancy dresses (left) for special events.

Dressed up in child-size versions of traditional costumes, Vinton Hooee and Tami Tsethlikai (left) walk down a path at Dowa Yalanne. But for everyday clothing, Zuni dress the way many other Westerners do (right) who work outside with horses and other livestock.

for weaving became available. The women's ceremonial outfit changed from a cotton dress to a woven dark blue one, with red designs along the bottom. This dress, called a *manta* (a Spanish word), is worn as an outer garment, with silk or some other slick material as an undergarment. White, wraparound moccasin "boots" made of buckskin complete the women's ceremonial clothes. Zuni men today typically dress in cowboy shirts, jeans, boots, and colorful head scarves or ten-gallon cowboy hats.

Houses

The first Zuni houses were built of stone with mud mortar, much the way today's adobe (sun-dried brick) houses are made in and around Santa Fe, New Mexico. Zuni houses were built two to six stories high, with small adjoining interior rooms. Ground-level doors or windows were not used. Higher levels were reached by movable outside ladders, which were removed during enemy attacks and at nighttime for security. Entrance into interior rooms was also by ladder.

In the old days Zuni houses were made of stone and mud mortar. They were clustered together, with ladders leading from level to level.

Areas of common use were on the first and second roof-top levels. Most rooms faced south to take full advantage of the Sun's warmth. Interior rooms were used for storing food. Those rooms were whitewashed, and outside walls were plastered with adobe mud.

Today one-story houses (right) are common. The Zuni have TVs, appliances, and often drive pickup trucks (below).

Houses were interconnected, with narrow alleyways between them leading to a central plaza. Historically, the main village of Zuni Pueblo was three to six stories high.

The modern Zuni village has all one-story houses, with ground-level doors and glass windows. Instead of stone and mud mortar, the houses are now usually made of cinder blocks or cut stone, with cement mortar. The Zuni have indoor plumbing, electricity, and all modern appliances, including television and telephone service.

Some Zuni also have double-wide mobile homes. Almost everyone has an automobile and depends on the supermarket for food.

Food

The primary crop of the A:shiwi in prehistoric times was "pod corn," a plant that looks like a wheat head with each kernel in its own husk. This was introduced into the Southwest sometime around 500 B.C. Corn, or maize, is a member of the grass family and is a cultigen—that is, each crop of it has to be planted, tended, and harvested at maturity.

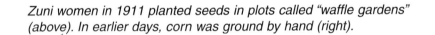

Zuni women in 1911 planted seeds in plots called "waffle gardens" (above). In earlier days, corn was ground by hand (right).

In the early days, good soil in the annual flood zones along stream and river courses was selected for planting. Since the Zuni then had no grazing animals, fences were not needed. Men planted and harvested the crops and provided the meat by hunting for wild game. They also gathered wood for cooking and warmth in the winter months. Women prepared the food, took care of the children, and tended to the houses.

Today the Zuni have adopted many foods from other cultures and have changed them for their own use. Some examples are **fry bread**, wheat pudding, **tortillas**, and **tamales**.

Arts and Crafts

There is no word for arts or crafts in the Zuni language. Containers for food, storage, paints, and cooking were first made for practical use. Shell, stone, and bone jewelry were decorative objects worn only on special ceremonial occasions.

Pottery-making was first introduced from Mexico in about A.D. 200. The Zuni soon developed their own special forms, designs, and styles. These special designs, unique to each culture, became the most reliable signs for tracing the movements of people throughout the Southwest.

Today Zuni decorated pottery is prized by people who collect it.

Chunks of turquoise from northern New Mexico were worn on necklaces and as earrings by both men and women. Seashells from the Gulf of Mexico and the Pacific Ocean were also made into beads and bracelets.

According to one story, the A:shiwi first learned the art of **silversmithing** from a Navajo man whose name was Atsiti Chon. Chon taught the art to a man named Laneyate. The first silversmithing tools were primitive and very limited, consisting of a **forge** and **bellows** made from a sheep or goat skin, a hammer, a small anvil, and a few large pot shards (broken pieces of pottery) for the **crucible**. The silversmith could only produce items of limited style and form.

Making silver jewelry has become an important craft and source of income for the Zuni.

The first A:shiwi silversmiths melted Mexican coins (pesos) and hammered them into small buttons, rings, bracelets, and other personal adornments. Early A:shiwi jewelry styles used turquoise as the focal point, whereas the Navajo silversmiths focused on metals.

In the late 1920s, white traders first came to the reservation. They created a market for Indian art, and the Indian "Artist." The A:shiwi quickly learned how much money they could make by adding an "Indian design" to a wire finger ring.

As artists acquired more advanced tools, their work became more refined. The addition of exotic minerals such as lapis lazuli, serpentine, and jet brought the art form to new heights. By 1947 the A:shiwi as a tribe made more money from their jewelry than from the sale of livestock and agriculture.

Turquoise and silver jewelry shine like a warm smile.

Today the A:shiwi excel as sculptors of Fetish charms, small stone images of fierce ancient animals turned to stone by A:shiwi gods. Fetishes are often sold as symbols of health and protection.

Lapis lazuli was used in this design that resembles Sun Father (left). Small stone animals called Fetishes (right), are some of the finest works by Zuni artists.

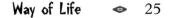

Spiritual Life

A:shiwi beliefs are based on an abiding respect for nature and the land. The Zuni believe that all the Earth serves as the sacred dwelling place of the spirit beings with whom we share this universe.

Zuni ceremonies are a complex fabric of dancing, singing, and prayers intended to keep the spirit beings happy. Each adult member of the tribe has a responsibility to help maintain and operate the universe on an even balance for the good of all people and for the joy of spirit beings.

As in other agricultural communities, the most ceremonially significant times are the summer and winter **solstices**. The summer solstice occurs at the end of June, in the middle of the ceremonial calendar. The winter solstice occurs 48 days after the new moon in the month of October.

In March 1998 Brandon Othole, then 12, performed the Turkey Dance for the public at the Indian Pueblo Cultural Center in Albuquerque, New Mexico.

26

Zuni dress in fine clothes for a ritual featuring corn. However, the people's spiritual life is lived every day, with or without ceremony.

The "New Fire" ceremony at the end of the 48 days is the actual end of the Zuni old year and the start of the new year. It is nearly the same time as the calendar new year that begins on January 1st.

The religion of the A:shiwi is not limited to a special day or ceremony. At any time and any place, an A:shiwi will offer a prayer and a gift of white cornmeal with crushed turquoise and seashells to Sun Father, Earth Mother, and the spirit beings. At every meal an A:shiwi will take a small portion of food, place it on the side of his or her plate, and speak the following:

"Here, grandfathers. You all eat. Add to your heart, and grant me long life."

An adult man also places a second portion on the side of his plate and adds the following:

"Here, Spirit Beings, you all eat. Add to your heart, and grant me long life."

The ancestors and spirit beings are fed at every meal. They are either fed on the plate, in the fireplace, or at the river.

Religious System

Zuni life, from birth until death, revolves around ritual. Many ceremonies and special observations mark the transition from one age or status to another.

The Zuni religious system includes the Rain Priest, the Medicine Societies, and the Bow Priests (described in the Tribal

Government section). The backbone of the Zuni religious system are the kivas, the sacred masked dance societies. All boys between the ages of eight and twelve are initiated into one of the six kiva groups. (Girls are not encouraged to join the societies because of the physically taxing initiation process.) After this initiation, the boy becomes an adult with adult religious responsibilities.

Zuni boys dance in public, wearing headdresses resembling the sacred white buffalo. In private they will join a kiva, or sacred masked dance society, and take on adult responsibilities.

Family Life

As children growing up, our grandfathers said to us: "Look, listen, learn, and remember; do not interrupt, be respectful. Be of good heart, be kind. You have only one beautiful life—love each other. Do not be destructive, and above all—do not be lazy. Someday you will be an elder, and through you will pass the history and traditions of our people."

—Zuni Tribal Elder

Clans

The clan system holds the entire village together. The system is matrilineal (clans trace their descent through the mother, not the father), matrilocal (the husband joins the bride's household), and exogamous (children cannot marry into their mother's or the father's clan). There are at present 21 Zuni clans.

When a child is born, regardless of its sex, it is born into the mother's clan, and of its father's clan. For example, a child is born to the Coyote clan and is a child of the Deer clan.

Julie, Alex, and Carlton Jamon are a family bound by the centuries-old system of clans. The system strengthens families and provides loving support.

Birthdays are not observed or celebrated in Zuni culture. The most attention a child will receive because of his or her birth is on the fourth day of life. The father's sister, the clan aunt, and the child's mother present the child to Sun Father. The child is then given its clan or family name (the father's clan relatives will support the child through every life crisis and prepare the child to return to the womb of Mother Earth upon death).

It is very impolite to ask anyone, "What is your name?" or call anyone by his or her name directly. You relate to them and call them by your relative age: younger brother, brother, younger sister, sister, grandmother, mother, or father—but never by name. There is one exception, however. You may use a person's English name. But you must never use your own name. It is considered rude and impolite.

A male child will receive a new and different name at initiation into one of the kiva societies. He will also get a third name if he joins a medicine society of healers.

Marriage Customs

Marriage within the mother's or father's clan is forbidden. When young people meet for the first time, they don't ask, "What is your name?" or "What tribe are you?" Instead they ask, "What is your clan?"

In the old days, the "coming together," or marriage, was an agreement between the young man, the young woman, and her family. A young man would first attempt to catch the attention of the young woman of his desire at various public events. When she discovered his interest, she would consult her mother. If the young man was found to be skillful, honest, of good heart, of the right clan, and from a good family, the mother would consent to her daughter's request to give the young man a sign of encouragement.

The two would meet "accidentally on purpose" a few times over the course of a month. Then the young man would move into the bride's household as a member of her family. During this time the new bride would grind corn flour to bring her new mother-in-law as a gift. In return the young man's mother would present her new daughter-in-law with a traditional women's outfit, formalizing the "coming together." Today many couples have a courtship and marriage ceremony similar to that of any Americans, although some traditions are still observed.

Clark and Bessie Coouancy have been married for many years, as have many older Zuni who value long lives together.

The Household

In earlier times, married women and their husbands and children formed the center of the household. The household included the mother, father, grandmother, grandfather, and unmarried males. The household was supported by the entire family. Older children took care of their younger brothers and

The Nahohai family (above), like many others, rely on relatives. In past times grandparents watched over grandchildren. That bond is still strong today (right).

sisters. Grandparents watched over all the children so that the older ones could do their work. Each generation was valued for its support and contributions. There were no day-care centers, no senior citizen centers, and there was no welfare. The home was built by the men in the family for the woman of the family. Women controlled all food supplies, the house, and the children. A typical Zuni family lived in a tidy room about 12 feet (4 m) by 14 feet (4.3 m). The adobe walls were neatly whitewashed. In the center stood a fireplace and chimney. Clothes hung from deer antlers or wooden pegs. Cooking was done in pots made of clay. Drinking water was kept in gourds, which also served as cups. Because corn was such an important part of the diet, girls had to spend three or four hours every day grinding it. When it was time to eat, family members took the blankets they were wearing, folded them up, and sat upon them. At night the family members slept in a row using the same blankets and perhaps a few robes made from rabbit skins.

It took many years to establish an independent household under the old system. This is no longer true. Today most young couples establish their own household from the start. But the same standards are necessary for marriage.

Tribal Government

Before the arrival of Spaniards, the six A:shiwi communities were joined together by a common language, the clan system, and their religious and ceremonial system. There was no king, chief, or absolute ruler of any kind. Each village was independent. Each had its own religious councils.

Some foreigners believe that Zuni society before 1540 was a theocracy (a culture ruled by its religious leaders). This is not so. The village religious councils made no laws or claims of divine guidance. Each directed the ceremonial system according to the traditions handed down from the "time of beginning."

The tribe's internal civil affairs were under the control and direction of the "Priest of the Bow," sometimes called the "War Chief." Bow Priests protected the people from intruders, enemy raids, and witchcraft. They represented the religious council in matters of state. Bow Priests conducted trials and sentenced those who performed religious and social taboos, or forbidden practices.

In 1873 the "Priest of the Bow," or "War Chief," stood like a tower of strength, ready to lead the Zuni Pueblo in all matters.

34

The Zuni had no jails. Crimes such as witchcraft were punishable by death or banishment. Individual or family cases were handled by the family. Crimes such as theft were also family matters that could be dealt with by the Priest of the Bow. Crimes against society, threats of death against an individual or a family, or, in rare cases, murder, were matters for the Spirit Beings to judge.

In the early 1900s, a political arm of the religious council was established to deal with the American government. A civil governor was selected by the religious council and installed for a one-year term. Prior to the 1940s, the tribal governor and councilmen were unpaid and selected for their status in the community and for their ability to work with outsiders. Women began to join the council in the 1960s, and three have served since then.

Today, in Zuni, candidates for governor campaign with their selection for lieutenant governor as a team. The governor is called Ta:pu:pu/u—meaning "the one who blows on wood." The wood refers to the cane, which is a symbol of authority for pueblo governors. It is a symbol that began with the Spanish, who gave the first canes to pueblo leaders. The tradition was continued by President Abraham Lincoln, when the Pueblo people came under jurisdiction of the U.S. as a result of war with Mexico. In 1864 President

In 1885 Palo-wa-ti-was was one of the last leaders of the Zuni under the old system.

Lincoln sent each of the pueblo governors a black, silver mounted cane to confirm their status as leaders of self-governing states. The Lincoln cane remains a cherished symbol of office and is passed on to each Zuni governor. The tribal governor and council are elected by popular vote every four years and are paid a regular salary. Their oath of office is given in a public ceremony by the Head Rain Priest of the East.

Certain religious matters are still directed and controlled by the Council of Religious Elders and the Bow Priest. But all issues from the outside concerning religious activities pass through the governor and tribal council for action. There is no direct contact between the outside world and the religious elders or the religious council. The Bow Priest speaks for the religious council. Any action with the outside world is taken through the tribal council.

Nontraditional churches on the reservation include a Christian Reform Mission Church and School, the St. Anthony Mission and School, a Church of Latter-Day Saints, and a Bahai temple.

Zuni Councilman Harry Chimoni stands in front of Corn Mountain. He worries that the use of groundwater by the nearby Fence Lake mine could disturb the process that produces salt in nearby Zuni Salt Lake.

Contemporary Life

Few Zunis volunteered for active duty during World War I, but during World War II, more than 300 young men out of a population of fewer than 6,000 Zunis were either drafted or volunteered for the Armed Forces. They fought in the European, Italian, and Pacific theaters of operation.

The postwar years saw many changes on the reservation. The U.S. government passed two bills to help returning servicemen. The "GI Bill" paid for veterans to attend college or technical schools. Many Zuni took advantage of the opportunity. Some trained in farm management and auto repair. Others worked toward higher degrees in education or **anthropology**.

A relocation program paid for servicemen and their families to move to one of the big industrial cities. Veterans received new jobs there, and housing was provided. But all the Zuni families that tried this program returned to their villages within five years. Without enough education, they simply could not compete. Today the A:shiwi have built up their own school district to solve that problem.

Since World War II, Zuni young people have studied hard, knowing that they have to "hit the books" to succeed in the modern world.

To race ahead these days, it is necessary to be fit and compete
in body as well as in mind.

Gallup, New Mexico, 40 miles north on Interstate 40, is the
nearest large town. It has food markets, gas stations, hardware
stores, cafés, a deli, a pizza parlor, and seven stores for buying
and selling arts and crafts. A modern hospital, two high schools,
two junior high schools, two grade schools, and a headstart
preschool provide services and courses, as does the University
of New Mexico, Gallup branch.

In the mid-1800s, **smallpox**, introduced by intruders from
the East, killed many of the Zuni. Only 1,120 of an estimated
15,000 people survived. The Zuni today have a population of
more than 10,000, a number that is rising steadily. Perhaps 9,000
live on the reservation, with the rest in nearby towns or attend-
ing various colleges, universities, or serving in the Armed Forces.

The Future

Today the Zuni face the same major problems as any society in the United States, including alcoholism and drug abuse. The reservation has a strong school system, and an excellent hospital for medical care.

Economically, the reservation is not large enough for those Zuni working as farmers to make a living. Income from agriculture and livestock is seasonal and at poverty levels according to U.S. government standards. The Zuni today work in the arts and crafts industry (mostly as silversmiths), in tribal government, in the sheep and cattle industry, or at off-reservation day jobs. Some work seasonally on forest fire-fighting crews.

Even if they live or work off the reservation, most Zuni return home frequently for ceremonial and religious occasions. As they did under Spanish rule, the A:shiwi have taken what they found useful from American society and adapted it for their own use. As one A:shiwi says: "We still have our language, our spiritual life ways, and our land base— that is, Our Culture."

Fun and fitness come together for a serious purpose: helping to fight the disease of diabetes.

Zuni Morning Prayer

ma/i:na melhi teje

lu/kaya yatonne

jon/a:wan yatokya tachu

yam telhashinakwin

yellanakwiak/a tuntekwin

ko:we an tew etchi kwi

yam ake a:shi/na yan a:te ona

towa k/ojan an jalawa tena ne

yam asin k/alhe akya

jo/ a:we yantena zume k/ana

lilha k/apinin a:jo/ a;wan

ona yalhan kwi na kwin

ton/a so a:wona: ela te kya

jom/ a:tachu k/apinn a: jo//i

la:jolhi le se te kwin

ton telhashinna/ulapan

a:te ona

/e lhi jom/ an jalawe tin nan ya/chi tan na me

yam ani kwanna akya

yam ik/ina kwi

yam shilh na kwi

/an na/kwa to k/anna

jo/na/a ton te k/ohanan e

ya nik chi ya:nap tu

/aki jo/lhi yam yatokya tachi an

ona:yanaka one yalhan kwi na:kwi n

ona:yalhi te/china/a

/i:ya/kana lho/o

/i: piya zumme

/an sam m/o

jon/n s len/akya /i:yon a: ya:k/anp tu

(English translation)

It is so
this day
our Sun Father
to your dwelling
you stand forth
nearly
with that of our completed flesh
sacred white prayer meal
with my warm hand
I grasp in strength
here the place of spirit beings
to their entrance
I have reached your road
my spirit fathers
In all directions
you reside all around
you are
do not my sacred prayer meal shun
with your spiritual power
to your heart
To your satisfaction
take into your body
with life
grant unto us
so that we Sun Father's
entrance of the complete road
we may reach
complete all
with strength
we all
we will thus complete our roads

Zuni Game

ta:sholi:we — "Wood Cards"

Any number of people can play this game. First you need 40 small stones, each 1 to 2 inches in diameter, and one flat stone, 8 to 10 inches across. Arrange the small stones in groups of ten in a circle, leaving about a 10-inch space between each group. These spaces are called "rivers." Place the flat stone in the center. This is the playing field.

The ta:sholi:we are made of three pieces of wood the same size—about 8 inches long, $1\frac{1}{2}$ inches wide, with a rounded surface on one side. The wood from an old apple crate is just about the right thickness. Paint each of the three pieces on the rounded side red.

Beginning the game of ta:sholi:we, or "wood cards."

42

Now the players each select a "horse." Your horse can be a red, green, or blue pencil, a twig from an apple tree, or anything that is different from the other players. Each player puts his or her horse into a selected "river" to start the game. Each player in turn (moving clockwise) folds and "bounces" the wood cards off the flat stone in the center to earn points. The number of points depends on how the cards land:

10 = All red gets an extra turn.
 5 = All white
 3 = Two red and one white
 2 = Two white and one red

A prize is agreed upon by the players. It is placed under the flat stone.

Players throw the cards to start. Whoever has the highest number of points goes first. The horses can move either left or right around the little circle of stones. The winner of the whole pot is the horse that enters the starting river on an even number. If a player is two stones away from the starting river and throws a three (two red and one white), he or she has to go completely around the circle again.

There are no ties or draws, and the winner takes all!

Zuni Chronology

5000–2500 B.C.	Paleo-Indian period. Big-game hunting, no permanent settlements.
2500 B.C.–A.D. 1	Archaic period. First attempts at agriculture.
A.D. 1–700	Development of pottery-making, pithouses.
900–1100	Development of painted pottery and pithouse villages. Settlement in Zuni area.
1300–1500	Six A:shiwi villages are founded.
1539	Esteban is killed at Hawikuh. Fray Marcos returns to Mexico City, and starts a "gold rush."
1540	Coronado arrives and battles with the A:shiwi.
1598	Juan de Oñate takes possession of all lands north of the Rio Grande River for Spain.
1680	The Pueblo Revolt.
1692	Don Diego de Vargas leads "Bloodless Reconquest."
1693–1700	Zunis vacate Corn Mountain. They consolidate their village into one site at Jalona:wa. This is the basis of the modern Zuni Pueblo.
1848	Treaty of Guadalupe Hidalgo is signed. The Zuni become part of the United States.
1853	A smallpox epidemic ravages the Zuni Pueblo, and thousands die.
1864	President Abraham Lincoln sends the Zuni governor a cane as a symbol of leadership. Giving the Zuni governor a cane confirmed in the eyes of the United States a line of succession that is now almost 400 years old.
1872	Zunis start using silver (coin silver) in their jewelry.

1877	The first Zuni reservation is established.
1924	Congress passes a law making all Indians citizens of the United States.
1925–1945	Silversmithing accounts for more than 50 percent of tribal income.
1934	Zunis vote to have popular elections for tribal officers.
1950	An electric power and water system is introduced into the village.
1970	The Zunis adopt a constitution.
1980	A Zuni Public School District is formed.
1990s	The Zuni Conservation project aims "to restore damaged Zuni lands and to protect and manage Zuni natural resources...."
	The Zuni Sustainable Agriculture Project aims to use both ancient and modern techniques to reduce erosion and retain water for irrigating (watering) crops. Zuni lands will then be more productive.

Glossary

Anthropology The study of human beings.

A:shiwi Zuni name for themselves. It has no English translation.

Bellows An instrument or machine that by expanding and contracting draws in air through a valve or hole and then expels it through a tube.

Crucible An earthen pot used for melting metals.

Forge A shop with a furnace where metal is heated and shaped.

Fry bread A quick bread cooked by deep-frying.

Hawikuh Ruins of one of the seven "cities of gold."

Jalona:itiwanna The historic "center place" of Zuni mythology; the modern Zuni village.

Jalona:wa The archaic name for the modern-day Zuni village.

Mesa A natural hill with steep sides and a flat top.

Silversmithing The art of working metals.

Smallpox A disease easily caught and often deadly that is caused by a virus. A person with smallpox has a high fever and pus-filled bumps on the skin that leave deep, permanent scars.

Solstice Either of two times of the year (in the summer and winter) when the Sun is at its greatest distance from the equator.

Tamales A dish made of fried chopped meat and crushed peppers, and lots of seasoning. They are rolled in cornmeal dough, wrapped in cornhusks, and steamed.

Tortillas Round, thin cakes made of cornmeal or wheat flour. They are usually eaten hot with a meat filling or topping.

Viceroy Most important Spanish colonial official; represents the king.

Yaaya A ceremonial dance during which the men and women hold hands.

Further Reading

Crampton, Gregory C. *The Zunis of Cibola.* University of Utah Press: Salt Lake City, Utah, 1977.

Ferguson T. J., and E. Richard Hart. *A Zuni Atlas.* University of Oklahoma Press: Norman and London, 1985.

Flanagan, Alice K. *The Zunis.* Children's Press, 1998.

Newman, Stanley. "Zuni Dictionary," *International Journal of American Linguistics,* Vol. 24, No. 1. Indiana University Research Center in Anthropological, Folklore, and Linguistics: Indiana, 1958.

Ortiz, Alfonso, editor. *Handbook of North American Indians.* Smithsonian Institution Press: Washington D.C., 1979.

Pollock, Penny. *The Turkey Girl: A Zuni Cinderella.* Little Brown, 1996.

Viola, Herman J. *North American Indians: An Introduction to the Lives of America's Native Peoples, from the Inuit of the Arctic to the Zuni of the Southwest.* Crown: New York, 1996.

Index

Numbers in italics indicate illustration or map.